Fish

Fish for fans

There is a good reason why fish has such an important place on the menus of the best and most famous restaurants – a place that is much more prominent than that of meat, poultry or game. Fish has many advantages. It is nutritionally rich, often inexpensive, immensely varied and easy to cook. Nothing succeeds as quickly and tastes as good as fish. Simply follow some important basic rules. Fish inspires delicious combinations with herbs, vegetables, cheese and a vast range of accompaniments. Let yourself be seduced by my recipe ideas – or go for your own! I wish you every success and a good appetite!

AURA

CONTENTS

3

Buy fish as fresh as possible

If possible, buy fish on the day you are going to cook it because it quickly loses its delicate flavour. This is particularly true of fine-textured fish, such as sole, plaice and salmon. If you keep fish any longer, its taste becomes more pronounced, which not everyone likes. Moreover, fish quickly 'goes off', so it should never be kept for long before cooking and eating. This means that fresh fish should be kept overnight only in exceptional circumstances and then, of course, you should store it in the refrigerator. It is best to lay it on a china plate and cover it loosely with greaseproof paper or foil to prevent the smell from permeating other food. This way, the fish does not become greasy, which can easily happen if it is completely wrapped in air-tight foil.

How can you tell if fish is fresh?

First of all, it is not in the interests of a fishmonger from whom you buy regularly or a supermarket chain to sell anything other than absolutely fresh fish. Nevertheless, it is always worth checking. In general, you can rely on your nose. Fresh fish does not have a powerful, 'fishy' odour, but a pleasant smell of the sea. The only exceptions are skate and shark, which have a faint smell of ammonia as a chemical called urea breaks down in their bodies. Allow one or two days after they have been caught before cooking skate or shark. Another sign, if you are buying whole fish rather than fillets, steaks or cutlets, is that the eyes should be clear and full with dark pupils and clear corneas. They should never be milky and sunken. The gills should be pink and the flesh should be springy and soft. The skin should have a damp gleam and be undamaged.

It is best to buy fish and seafood on the day you want to cook it. Fish loses its flavour and texture if it is stored for long.

Alternatives to fresh fish

If you cannot get fresh fish, frozen fish is the ideal alternative. It is useful to keep a supply in the freezer: most supermarkets usually stock frozen cod, haddock and plaice divided into portions, cleaned and filleted. These varieties are suitable for almost every kind of cooking. For special recipes you can also buy frozen salmon, trout, sole, whole sardines and even unusual tropical fish. It is important to thaw frozen fish as slowly as possible, ideally in the refrigerator, to ensure that its flavour and texture are as good as fresh fish. This also applies to seafood, such as mussels, crab and prawns, which are available fresh and frozen, too.

You can, of course, freeze fresh fish yourself, provided you do so on the day you buy it. However, it is important to be sure that the fish has not already been frozen at sea and then thawed for sale. The rule that you should never re-freeze raw ingredients applies to fish, too. You can freeze a dish that you have prepared and cooked from frozen fish.

You can keep smoked fish for a few days in the refrigerator, although it tastes best if it is bought when very fresh. Keeping it in the refrigerator will prevent its going off, but the delicious smoky flavour is lost after a short time. Some smoked fish, such as smoked salmon and kippers, is also available frozen. Vacuum-packed smoked fish will keep for two or three days longer in the refrigerator and can also be frozen on the day of purchase.

You do not really have any storage problems with canned fish. It is fully preserved and so will actually keep for years, even without being refrigerated. However, you should take notice of the 'use-by' date, which is always clearly marked on the can. Once opened, canned fish will deteriorate rapidly.

Canned fish is ideal for store-cupboard cooking and for salads, sandwiches and snacks. If you are counting calories, buy canned fish in brine, rather than in oil. As well as tuna, sardines, salmon and other varieties are sold in this form.

How much fish per person?

If fish is to be the main course, you will need 200–250 g/ 7–9 oz of filleted fish per person or 300 g/11 oz of unfilleted fish per person. Allow 250 g/9 oz fish steaks or cutlets per person. (Steaks are cut from the tail end of round fish, while cutlets are cut from the centre.) Single portion fish, such as trout, snapper or mackerel, should weigh 300–450 g/11 oz–1 lb.

If there are any leftovers, wonderful! You can use them for a delicious starter. Arrange the pieces of fish on a bed of mixed salad leaves, such as lollo rosso, escarole, oak leaf lettuce and frisée. Sprinkle with a little balsamic vinegar, lemon juice and olive oil. Scatter over a few chopped fresh herbs and season sparingly with salt and pepper. Add any extras you like, such as tomatoes, cucumber, blanched green beans, artichoke hearts or olives. This is better than mixing the fish leftovers with the salad, because then the fish tends to disintegrate.

Preparing fish is quick and easy

Gutting, scaling, and filleting are best left to the fishmonger, if possible. Professionals have experience and the proper tools, such as razor-sharp filleting knives, scaling knives and high-pressure water hoses with which to wash the fish spotlessly clean, both inside and out. They will almost certainly do this fairly unpleasant job more neatly and much faster than you will yourself. Another advantage of buying cleaned fish ready for cooking is that it remains fresh longer.

You will not have much left to do at home until you start cooking. Rinse the fish again in cold running water and pat it thoroughly dry with kitchen paper. This is particularly important when you want to fry it in breadcrumbs. Breadcrumbs will not stick to wet fish and it will not fry to a crisp golden crust.

The classic three-point rule for fish

This rule states 'clean, sour and salt'. Nowadays, following this instruction is not so important. Cleaning is now usually unnecessary, as the fishmonger will already have done it for you. Gourmets and, indeed, fish-lovers dispute the need to make fish sour, particularly the delicate varieties, such as sole, plaice and salmon. Of course, a few drops of lemon juice do not hurt these fish either, but too much sourness can destroy the delicate flavour. Instead of adding lemon or vinegar, you could try orange or lime juice. They are not so sour and give the fish an exquisite taste. In fact wine, which is a common ingredient in many classic fish dishes, is usually 'sour' enough in itself. Fish cooked in wine will certainly not taste insipid!

You should also be sparing with salt. A pinch is often enough. Sea fish, in particular, are often naturally salty. Use a good-quality sea salt, which has more flavour than ordinary table salt and contains important trace elements, such as iodine. You should also be sparing with spices, particularly those that are very strong or hot. It is easy to mask the fish's own taste. The exact opposite is true of herbs. You can use fresh herbs as generously as you like. They go wonderfully with all fish and do not destroy its flavour. Parsley and dill are classic seasonings for fish, but other herbs, such as chervil, fennel, marjoram and mint, also impart a special flavour.

Cook gently for a short time

You may well not agree with the current trend for cooking fish for such a short time that it remains raw and transparent in the centre around the bone. Nevertheless, it should never be cooked for longer than necessary. This dries out the flesh and a tender, moist fish can easily become tough, tasteless and rubbery.

Exact cooking times are given in the recipes that follow. You can also use them as a guide when you are experimenting with your own fish creations. If you are in any doubt, it is better to remove the fish from the hob or oven a little sooner than suggested and leave it to stand, with the lid on, for a further 5–10 minutes to finish cooking. This gentle method suits the fish better than aggressive direct heat.

Wine is an ingredient in many recipes. If you do not want to use alcohol, you can replace it with good-quality fish or vegetable stock.

The most important cooking methods

<u>Poaching</u>

No fish should be boiled vigorously. It would quickly fall to pieces and lose all its flavour. To poach fish, the liquid should simmer very gently over a low heat. Fish may be poached in fish or vegetable stock, milk, plain water or with the addition of wine, lemon juice or vinegar.

The classic poaching liquid for fish is a *court-bouillon*, an aromatic stock. You will need 3 litres/5¼ pints water, a mixture of finely chopped or, better still, grated root vegetables, such as carrots, celery, leeks and onions, plus a few fresh herbs, such as parsley, thyme or bay leaves, 2.5 ml/ ½ teaspoon whole white peppercorns and 5–10 ml/

Canned fish, from sardines, anchovies and tuna to clams, mussels and prawns, is ideal for store-cupboard cooking.

1–2 teaspoons sea salt. Avoid any vegetables or herbs that are very strong-tasting, as the fish will absorb the flavours of the *court-bouillon*. Boil the stock vigorously for about 30 minutes. Ideally, the *court-bouillon* should then be allowed to cool before using, but if you are in a hurry, you can simply lower the heat, add the fish and simmer until cooked. Fish fillets take about 8 minutes, while a large, whole fish can take up to 1 hour.

Cooking *au bleu*

This classic method of cooking works only with whole fish that have an undamaged membrane on their skin. Varieties traditionally cooked in this way include trout, carp and pike. Extremely fresh fish are plunged into a *court-bouillon* containing vinegar and then poached in it.

To cook trout *au bleu*, add 75 ml/5 tablespoons good-quality, white wine vinegar to 1 litre/1¾ pints *court-bouillon*. Poach the fish in this liquid as usual until it is cooked. During this process it turns to a shining, metallic blue colour. Cooking this way does not greatly influence the taste, but the fish looks absolutely spectacular when served!

To succeed with this method, handle the fish as little as possible and hold it very gently when you unwrap and prepare it to avoid damaging the membrane. Then there will be

Classic ingredients for fish dishes are lemon juice, wine and fresh herbs. In addition, if you fry fish, you will hardly be able to do without onions.

no gaps in the final blue colour and the fish will not be spotty.

If you want a particularly intense blue colour, bring 400 ml/14 fl oz white wine vinegar to the boil, together with 105 ml/7 tablespoons water. Pour this concentrated vinegar solution over the raw fish. Set aside for 1 minute and then cook it in the normal cooking liquid.

Steaming

This is a wonderful method for gently cooking delicate fish fillets or whole fish and, at the same time, gives them a particularly fine flavour. It also

preserves valuable nutrients. Add some aromatic drink, such as white wine, sherry or vermouth, to a liquid in which you have already boiled fresh herbs and/or vegetables. Pour this liquid into the base of a steamer and place the fish in the top. You can also simply put the fish on a plate and rest this on top of an upturned cup so that it is not actually immersed in the aromatic liquid. Large fish can be steamed on a grid resting in a roasting tin. Whichever method you use, make sure that the fish cooks in the steam which rises from heating the liquid, not in the liquid itself.

Braising

This cooking method is suitable for all kinds of fish, either whole or filleted, and for cutlets and steaks. It is also practical because it creates a delicious sauce all by itself. The principle is always the same. Fry onions or shallots and, perhaps, garlic in hot oil. Add more vegetables, such as mushrooms, tomatoes or spinach. You can use anything that does not take too long to cook and has enough natural juices. Arrange the fish on top of the vegetables, season and cook on the hob or in a preheated oven at 180°C/350°F/Gas 4. This cooking method has endless variations and is very suitable for beginners because not much can go wrong.

Frying and deep-frying

Fried fish is delicious if it is really crisp all over. When frying, make sure you do not burn it or let it dry out, which can happen if the heat is too high. On the other hand, do not let it absorb too much oil, which happens if the heat is too low. This requires experience. If you are unsure, you can try this trick: fry the fish on both sides in the frying pan only until it is nicely golden brown. Then finish off cooking it through in the oven at 190°C/375°F/Gas 5.

You can ensure that fried fish is particularly crisp if you dry it well before cooking and coat it in flour or in egg and breadcrumbs. It tastes even more delicious if you add finely chopped nuts, sesame seeds, chopped herbs or cheese to the breadcrumb mixture.

For deep-fat frying, the fish is usually coated in batter or breadcrumbs to protect it. This method is particularly suitable for small fish, such as whitebait and sardines, and for firm fish fillets, such as cod and halibut.

For the batter, mix together 250 g/9 oz flour, 2 eggs, salt and enough beer or wine to make a smooth liquid. Set aside for about 20 minutes. Pat the fish dry with kitchen paper and carefully dip each piece in the batter until it is coated all over. Fry immediately in hot oil until it turns golden brown. Serve with slices of lemon. This method also works well with squid rings and prawns.

Grilling

This is probably one of the earliest ways of cooking fish and, for many, it remains the best. You will not get the same results as on an outdoor barbecue, but even fish grilled

The right pots and pans make everything easier. You will find an abundant choice of tools and equipment in supermarkets, department stores and cookware shops. A fish kettle is ideal for poaching whole fish. The fish rests on a trivet and the lid is tight-fitting. Place the kettle over two hob rings or in the oven.

in the ordinary way at home is absolutely delicious.

There are two methods. You can grill the fish without any wrapping. This is suitable for oily fish, such as mackerel, sardines, herring and salmon cutlets or steaks. Brush the fish well with vegetable oil, so that they do not stick to the grill and season with salt and pepper only when they are cooked. This keeps them juicier.

A second method is suitable for more delicate fish, such as trout, salmon trout, sea bream and red mullet. Marinate the fish for a day in a mixture of olive oil, wine vinegar, chopped onions, chopped fresh herbs, a little sugar and salt. Wrap each fish, with a little marinade, in its own aluminium foil parcel. Then grill it on both sides. You can also wrap the fish in vine leaves or blanched cabbage leaves. This tastes delicious and looks very decorative.

Cooking in salt

This is a simple, but exquisite cooking method, traditionally used with sea fish. Your guests will be thrilled with fish served in a glittering salt crust. However, it is not just a delight for the eyes. The fish, enclosed in salt, remains juicy and full of flavour. This method is suitable only for whole fish. The skin protects it from soaking up the salt. Use coarse sea salt for the crust. For 1 kg/2¼ lb of fish you need 1.5–2 kg/3½–4½ lb salt. See recipe on page 54.

Fish stock

Whenever you buy fresh fish and ask the fishmonger to fillet it, take the skin, bones and heads with you. Cook them to give you the perfect base for a tasty fish stock, a delicious fish soup or an exquisite sauce to go with fish.

Basic fish stock

Rinse 1 kg/2¼ lb fish trimmings and put them into a large saucepan with several coarsely chopped root vegetables, 1 bunch fresh parsley, a few sprigs fresh thyme, bay leaves, 15 ml/1 tablespoon white peppercorns and 2.5 ml/ ½ teaspoon salt. Pour in 2 litres/3½ pints water (or half water, half white wine). Bring the mixture to the boil and skim of the scum. Simmer over a low heat for 45 minutes. Strain and set aside to cool. Freeze in small containers, such as yogurt pots. Then you can thaw and use the amount you want when you need it.

You can also make a delicious shellfish stock from prawn heads and shells.

Fish is so healthy

Nutritionists have long been recommending it. For a really healthy diet, you should eat fish at least twice a week, not just on Fridays or particular feast days. Fish is low in calories, easily digestible and rich in valuable protein and essential vitamins and minerals. Even more important, because of its high content of unsaturated fats, it is thought to help lower the body's cholesterol. For example, among Eskimos, who live almost exclusively on fish (including very oily fish), the diseases of our society, such as arteriosclerosis and heart attacks, are almost unknown.

So you can see there are many reasons for eating fish and seafood – not only because they taste so delicious.

The best drink to go with a fish or seafood dish is usually a sharp, dry white wine. So here's wishing you *bon appetit!*

Fish cooked in a sea salt coating is not just spectacular to look at, but also has an exquisite flavour.

Scampi and avocado pears

For guests

Serves 4
16 fresh scampi or langoustines
2 ripe avocado pears
juice of 1 lemon
2 beef tomatoes
2 shallots
45 ml/3 tablespoons white
   wine vinegar
5 ml/1 teaspoon Dijon or other
   mild mustard
freshly ground white pepper
75 ml/5 tablespoon olive oil
salt
toasted French bread, to serve

Approximately per portion:
1,600 kj/380 kcal
18 g protein
32 g fat
5 g carbohydrate
● Approximate preparation time: 40 minutes

1. Place the scampi or langoustines in a medium-size saucepan. Add sufficient boiling water just to cover and cook for 2–3 minutes. Drain and set aside to cool.

2. Peel the avocado pears, cut in half and remove the stones. Finely dice the flesh and sprinkle immediately with lemon juice to prevent discolouration.

3. Blanch the beef tomatoes in boiling water for 1–2 minutes, Drain, skin and cut in half crossways. Remove the seeds and finely dice the flesh.

4. Finely chop the shallots. Place the avocado pears, tomatoes and shallots in a salad bowl.

5. Mix together the white wine vinegar, mustard, pepper and olive oil to make a creamy dressing. Season to taste with salt. Pour the dressing over the avocado mixture and toss the salad.

6. Peel and devein the scampi or langoustines and remove their heads. Mix the scampi into the salad and serve with toasted French bread.

Tip

To peel and devein seafood, such as scampi and prawns, remove the head by pulling it between the index finger and thumb of one hand, while holding the body with the other hand. Carefully loosen the shell from the meat and remove it. Slit the body along the back with a sharp, pointed knife. Pull out the black thread that runs along it with the knife point.

Smoked fish salad

Exquisite

Serves 4
250 g/9 oz button mushrooms
juice of 1 lemon
2 shallots
350 g/12 oz smoked fish, such as
   mackerel or buckling
60 ml/4 tablespoons white
   wine vinegar
salt
freshly ground white pepper
freshly grated nutmeg
4 tablespoons sunflower oil
2 spring onions
1 small lettuce

Approximately per portion:
1,500 kj/360 kcal
21 g protein
29 g fat
3 g carbohydrate
● Approximate preparation time: 40 minutes

1. Thinly slice the button mushrooms and sprinkle with lemon juice immediately.

2. Finely chop the shallots. Skin the smoked fish and cut into slices about 5 mm/¼ inch thick. Put the shallots, fish slices and mushrooms into a bowl.

3. Mix the white wine vinegar with salt, pepper and nutmeg to taste. Beat in the oil with a whisk until it makes a creamy dressing. Pour the dressing over the fish and mushroom mixture. Toss the salad thoroughly and set aside for about 10 minutes.

4. Meanwhile, thinly slice the spring onions into tiny rings. Add them to the salad. Adjust the seasoning, if necessary.

5. Divide the lettuce leaves between 4 individual plates. Spoon over the smoked fish mixture and serve the salad.

Above: Scampi and avocado pears
Below: Smoked fish salad

Monkfish carpaccio

Exclusive

Serves 4
600 g/1 lb 5 oz monkfish fillets
2 bunches fresh flat leaf parsley
½ bunch fresh thyme
½ bunch fresh oregano
90 g/3½ oz can anchovy fillets
1 garlic clove
250 ml/8 fl oz olive oil
salt
freshly ground black pepper
15 ml/1 tablespoon brandy
toasted white bread triangles and
*   sparkling white wine (optional),*
*   to serve*

Approximately per portion:
3,300 kj/790 kcal
33 g protein
71 g fat
1 g carbohydrate

● Approximate preparation
   time: 2½ hours (2 hours are
   chilling time

---

1. Remove any small bones from the monkfish fillet with tweezers. Wrap the fish in foil and put it in the freezer for about 2 hours.

2. Pull the parsley, thyme and oregano leaves off the stalks.

3. Rinse the anchovy fillets in cold water and pat dry. Put the parsley, thyme, oregano, anchovies, garlic and 200 ml/7 fl oz of the olive oil in a food processor and work to a purée. Season with salt and pepper to taste and stir in the brandy.

4. Remove the monkfish from the freezer and cut into wafer-thin slices with an electric carving knife or a very sharp knife.

5. Brush the remaining olive oil over 4 individual serving plates. Arrange the monkfish slices on them in the form of rosettes and spoon the sauce on to the side. Serve with toast and sparkling white wine, if liked.

Tip

Before preparing the monkfish fillets, test for any remaining bones. Pull these out carefully with tweezers without damaging the flesh.

Prawn salad

Serves 4
115 g/4 oz cellophane noodles
1 large leek
2 carrots
salt
45 ml/3 tablespoons white
*   wine vinegar*
freshly ground black pepper
45 ml/3 tablespoons sesame oil
15 ml/1 tablespoon lemon juice
1 cm/½ inch piece fresh root ginger
350 g/12 oz cooked, peeled prawns

Approximately per portion:
1,000 kj/240 kcal
20 g protein
9 g fat
22 g carbohydrate

● Approximate preparation
   time: 30 minutes

---

1. Soak the cellophane noodles in boiling water for about 5 minutes. Drain, rinse in cold water and drain well again. Cut up the noodles with kitchen scissors.

2. Meanwhile, cut the leek in half lengthways, and then crossways into matchstick strips.

3. Finely dice the carrots. Blanch the carrots and leek in lightly salted, boiling water for about 1 minute. Refresh in iced water and drain well.

4. Mix the vinegar with salt and pepper to taste. Add the oil and lemon juice. Grate the ginger and add to the dressing.

5. Put the noodles, vegetables and prawns into a serving bowl. Pour over the dressing and toss well together. Set aside in the refrigerator for about 15 minutes, then serve.

Variation
You can also make this salad with 350 g/12 oz cooked crabmeat.

Tip

Sesame oil gives the salad a wonderful flavour. You can buy it in Chinese food stores and some supermarkets.

Above: Monkfish carpaccio
Below: Prawn salad

Scallops in cider sauce

Exclusive

Serves 4
3 shallots
25 g/1 oz butter
1 garlic clove
250 ml/8 fl oz dry cider
200 ml/7 fl oz double cream
salt
freshly ground white pepper
cayenne pepper
5 ml/1 teaspoon lemon juice
500 g/1 ¼ lb shelled scallops,
  corals reserved
¼ bunch fresh sorrel or chervil
boiled rice, to serve

Approximately per portion:
1,400 kj/330 kcal
14 g protein
23 g fat
8 g carbohydrate

● Approximate preparation
  time: 30 minutes

Tip

To open a scallop, hold firmly with the flat shell upwards. Using a short knife, probe between the shells to find an opening, then insert the blade and run it across the inside of the top shell. Gently lever the shells apart with the knife blade and separate with your hands. Loosen the scallop with the knife. Cut away and use the white muscle and pink coral.

1. Finely chop the shallots. Melt the butter in a large frying pan with high sides. Add the shallots and fry over a low heat for 2–3 minutes. Crush the garlic, add it to the pan and fry for a further 1 minute.

2. Pour in the cider, bring to the boil and cook until it has reduced by about half. Stir in the cream and simmer over a low heat until the sauce thickens. Transfer the mixture to a food processor and work to form a purée. Season with salt, white pepper and cayenne pepper to taste and stir in the lemon juice.

3. If the corals are still attached to the scallops, carefully remove them and set aside. Return the sauce to the frying pan. Add the scallops, cover and cook over a low heat for about 3 minutes.

4. Reserve a few sorrel or chervil leaves for the garnish and cut the remainder into thin strips. Add the sorrel or chervil strips and the corals to the sauce and cook for a further 1–2 minutes, until heated through. Transfer to 4 individual serving plates, garnish with the reserved herbs and serve immediately with rice.

Pickled herrings in red wine

Rather time-consuming

Serves 4
8 herring fillets
8 gherkins
2 small red onions
5 ml/1 teaspoon mustard seeds
5 ml/1 teaspoon pink peppercorns
salt
4 allspice berries
1 bay leaf
15 ml/1 tablespoon clear honey
150 ml/¼ pint dry red wine
105 ml/7 tablespoons red
  wine vinegar
fresh basil sprigs and cherry
  tomatoes, to garnish
brown bread, to serve

Approximately per portion:
1,800 kj/430 kcal
21 g protein
29 g fat
6 g carbohydrate

- Approximate preparation
  time: 45 minutes

- Marinating time: 12 hours

1. Cut the herring fillets and gherkins in half lengthways. Roll up 1 gherkin half in each herring half and fasten each roll with a cocktail stick. Arrange the rolls in a single layer in a large dish.

2. Thinly slice the onions and push out into rings. Arrange the onion rings evenly over the herring rolls. Set aside.

3. Put the mustard seeds, peppercorns and a pinch of salt into a saucepan. Add the allspice berries, bay leaf, honey, red wine and red wine vinegar. Bring to the boil and simmer over a low heat for about 20 minutes.

4. Set the liquid aside to cool for about 10 minutes, then pour it over the herring rolls. Cover the dish with a lid or aluminium foil and set aside in the refrigerator for about 12 hours. Arrange the pickled herrings on a serving dish, garnish with the basil sprigs and cherry tomatoes and serve with brown bread.

Mackerel mousse

Easy to make

Serves 4
250 g/9 oz smoked mackerel fillets
15 ml/1 tablespoon crème fraîche
2 egg yolks
salt
freshly ground white pepper
cayenne pepper
5 ml/1 teaspoon lemon juice
30 ml/2 tablespoons white
   wine vinegar
2 tablespoons sunflower oil
1 small frisée lettuce
4 small tomatoes
toasted brown bread and butter,
   to serve

Approximately per portion:
790 kj/190 kcal
13 g protein
14 g fat
3 g carbohydrate

● Approximate preparation
   time: 1½ hours (1 hour
   chilling time)

---

1. Skin the mackerel fillets, place in a food processor and work to a smooth purée. Transfer the purée to a bowl and mix in the crème fraîche and the egg yolks. Season with salt, white pepper and cayenne pepper and mix in the lemon juice. Cover and set aside in the refrigerator for about 1 hour.

2. Mix together the vinegar and oil and season with salt and white pepper to taste to make a creamy dressing. Toss the lettuce in the dressing and arrange on 4 individual serving plates. Cut the tomatoes in half and divide them between the plates.

3. Using a teaspoon, shape the mackerel mousse into small ovals. Arrange these decoratively on the plates. Serve with toasted brown bread and butter.

Variation
You could also make this mousse using any smoked oily fish, such as kippers or buckling.

Pastry crab rolls

Exclusive

Makes 12 rolls
450 g/1 lb frozen puff pastry dough
1 small onion
45 ml/3 tablespoons groundnut oil
250 g/9 oz beansprouts
1 cm/½ inch piece fresh root ginger
30–45 ml/2–3 tablespoons light
   soy sauce
200 ml/7 fl oz dry sherry
salt
freshly ground black pepper
chilli powder
1 bunch of fresh flat leaf parsley
250 g/9 oz cooked crabmeat
2 egg yolks

Approximately per roll:
800 kj/190 kcal
7 g protein
12 g fat
14 g carbohydrate

● Approximate preparation
   time: 1 hour

---

1. Thaw the puff pastry, following the instructions on the packet.

2. Finely chop the onion. Heat the oil in a large frying pan. Add the onion and fry over a medium heat for 3–5 minutes, until soft.

3. Rinse the beansprouts in cold running water. Finely chop the ginger. Add the beansprouts and ginger to the frying pan. Add the soy sauce and sherry and cook over a low heat for about 10 minutes. Remove from the heat and season to taste with salt, pepper and chilli powder.

4. Preheat the oven to 200°C/400°F/Gas 6. Pull the parsley leaves off the stalks and chop coarsely. Coarsely chop the crabmeat. Mix the parsley and crabmeat with the vegetables in the frying pan.

5. Roll out the pastry into rectangles double the size you need and cut them across once. Divide the crab mixture between the pieces of dough. Fold in the longer edges and roll up from the short end, pressing gently where the edges meet to seal. Rinse a baking sheet with cold water and arrange the rolls on it, seam side down, in a single layer.

6. Lightly beat the egg yolks and use to brush the rolls to glaze. Bake the rolls in the oven for 15–20 minutes. Remove from the oven and serve warm or cold.

Variation
You can also make these pastry rolls with 250 g/9 oz cooked, peeled prawns.

Above: Mackerel mousse
Below: Pastry crab rolls

Herring salad

Quick • Easy to make

Serves 4
8 herring fillets
2 onions
2 small cooking apples
250 ml/8 fl oz soured cream
45 ml/3 tablespoons lemon juice
salt
freshly ground white pepper
cayenne pepper
1 bunch fresh dill
1 bunch radishes

Approximately per portion:
2,000 kj/480 kcal
24 g protein
36 g fat
12 g carbohydrate

● Approximate preparation
  time: 25 minutes

1. Cut the fish into strips and place in a bowl. Finely chop the onions and add them to the fish.

2. Quarter, core and slice the apples, then add them to the fish. Pour the soured cream and lemon juice over the fish mixture. Season to taste with salt, white pepper and cayenne pepper and mix.

3. Reserve a few dill sprigs for the garnish. Remove the stalks from the remainder and finely chop the leaves. Thinly slice the radishes. Reserve a few slices and mix the remainder into the salad, together with the chopped dill. Divide the salad between 4 individual serving plates and serve, garnished with the reserved dill and radish slices.

Fish terrine

Rather time-consuming

Serves 8
3 shallots
25 g/1 oz butter
1 small courgette
600 g/1 lb 5 oz cod fillets
juice of ½ lemon
salt
freshly ground white pepper
pinch of cayenne pepper
freshly grated nutmeg
250 ml/8 fl oz double cream
2 egg yolks
250 g/9 oz spinach
200 g/7 oz salmon trout
vegetable oil, for brushing
mixed salad, to serve

Approximately per portion:
940 kj/220 kcal
20 g protein
15 g fat
2 g carbohydrate

● Approximate preparation
  time: 2 hours

● Cooling time: 4 hours

1. Finely chop the shallots. Melt the butter in a frying pan. Add the shallots and fry for 2–3 minutes. Grate the courgette, add to the pan and cook over a low heat, stirring occasionally, for 8 minutes.

2. Skin the cod fillets and cut into pieces. Sprinkle with lemon juice and transfer to a food processor. Add the courgette mixture and work to make a purée. Season to taste with salt, white pepper, cayenne pepper and nutmeg.

3. Beat the cream until it is stiff. Fold it into the fish mixture, together with the egg yolks.

4. Blanch the spinach in boiling salted water for 1 minute, drain, refresh in cold water and drain again. Dampen a tea cloth and lay the spinach leaves on it, over-lapping, to form a rectangle the same length as and a little wider than loaf tin you are going to use.

5. Cut the salmon trout into 2 cm/¾ inch slices and arrange them on the spinach. Lift the cloth on one side and fold half the spinach over the top of the fish so that it is wrapped all round in spinach.

6. Preheat the oven to its lowest setting. Line a 1 kg/2¼ lb loaf tin with aluminium foil and brush it with vegetable oil. Spoon in half the cod mixture and smooth the surface. Arrange the spinach roll on top and then spoon in the remaining cod mixture. Smooth the surface.

7. Cover the loaf tin securely with aluminium foil and stand it in a roasting tin. Add sufficient hot water to come halfway up the sides of the loaf tin and bake in the oven for about 35 minutes. Remove the tin from the oven and discard the foil covering. Return it to the oven for a further 35 minutes.

8. Set the terrine aside to cool for about 4 hours. Turn it out of the tin, cut it into slices and serve with a mixed salad.

Above: Herring salad
Below: Fish terrine

Smoked trout soup

For guests

Serves 4
2 smoked trout (each about 250 g/9 oz)
1 small onion
1.5 litres/2½ pints water
120 ml/4 fl oz double cream
2 egg yolks
15 ml/1 tablespoon lemon juice
salt
freshly ground white pepper
Worcestershire sauce
40 g/1½ oz fresh chervil
toast white bread and butter, to serve

Approximately per portion:
910 kj/220 kcal
21 g protein
13 g fat
2 g carbohydrate

● Approximate preparation time: 1¼ hours

1. Skin the trout, cut it into fillets and set all but one aside. Cut the remaining fillet into bite-size pieces and set aside. Reserve the skin and bones for making the stock.

2. Cut the onion into quarters and put it into a large saucepan, together with the fish skin and bones. Pour in the water and bring to the boil. Reduce the heat and simmer over a low heat for about 35 minutes, until the liquid has reduced by a third. Strain and return the stock to the saucepan. Discard the onion and trimmings.

3. Put the whole trout fillets and cream in a food processor and work to make a smooth purée. Add the purée to the saucepan and bring to the boil.

4. Place about 15–30 ml/1–2 tablespoons of the fish cooking liquid in a small bowl, add the egg yolks and lightly beat together. Stir the mixture into the soup and cook over a medium heat until thickened, but do not allow to boil. Carefully stir in the reserved trout pieces.

5. Stir in the lemon juice and season the soup to taste with salt, pepper, and Worcestershire sauce. Pull the chervil leaves off the stems. Ladle the soup into 4 individual soup bowls, garnish with the chervil and serve with buttered toast.

Hungarian fish soup

Traditional recipe

Serves 4
1 kg/2¼ lb mixed freshwater fish, such as pike, carp and trout, cleaned and with heads reserved
3 large onions
400 g/14 oz firm potatoes
4 beef tomatoes
30 ml/2 tablespoons sunflower oil
30 ml/2 tablespoons mild paprika
120 ml/4 fl oz fish stock
salt
freshly ground black pepper
2 green peppers
4 slices white bread

Approximately per portion:
1,700 kj/400 kcal
43 g protein
12 g fat
36 g carbohydrate

● Approximate preparation time: 1½ hours

1. Cut the fish into bite-size pieces.

2. Finely chop the onions and dice the potatoes. Blanch the tomatoes in boiling water for 1–2 minutes, drain, skin and remove the pips. Coarsely chop the flesh.

3. Heat the oil in a large saucepan. Add the onions and potatoes and fry over a low heat for about 10 minutes. Sprinkle over the paprika and stir in the tomatoes.

4. Pour the fish stock into the saucepan and bring to the boil. Season to taste with salt and pepper. Add the fish heads, cover and simmer over a low heat for about 30 minutes. Remove and discard the fish heads.

5. Meanwhile, core and seed the green peppers and cut into strips.

6. Add the fish and green peppers to the saucepan, cover and cook over a low heat for about 10 minutes.

7. Place 1 slice of white bread in the base of each of 4 individual soup plates, ladle over the fish soup and serve immediately.

Above: Hungarian fish soup
Below: Smoked trout soup

Friesian fish soup

Rather time-consuming

Serves 4
1 kg/2¼ lb mixed sea fish, such as
    haddock, cod, monkfish
    and plaice
1 carrot
1 onion
1 leek
¼ head of celery
300 g/11 oz fish trimmings
15 ml/1 tablespoon white
    peppercorns
1 bay leaf
250 ml/8 fl oz dry white wine
750 ml/1¼ pints water
3 egg yolks
250 ml/8 fl oz double cream
salt
freshly ground white pepper
5 ml/1 teaspoon lemon juice
1 bunch fresh dill

Approximately per portion:
1,900 kj/450 kcal
47 g protein
23 g fat
8 g carbohydrate

● Approximate preparation
  time: 1¼ hours

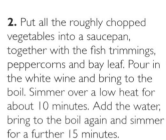

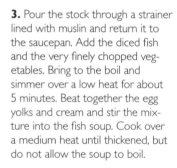

1. If necessary, skin and bone the fish. Then cut into bite-size pieces. Cut the carrot, onion and leek in half. Roughly chop one half and very finely chop the other half of each. Divide the celery in half and roughly chop one half and very finely chop the other.

2. Put all the roughly chopped vegetables into a saucepan, together with the fish trimmings, peppercorns and bay leaf. Pour in the white wine and bring to the boil. Simmer over a low heat for about 10 minutes. Add the water, bring to the boil again and simmer for a further 15 minutes.

3. Pour the stock through a strainer lined with muslin and return it to the saucepan. Add the diced fish and the very finely chopped vegetables. Bring to the boil and simmer over a low heat for about 5 minutes. Beat together the egg yolks and cream and stir the mixture into the fish soup. Cook over a medium heat until thickened, but do not allow the soup to boil.

4. Season the soup with salt and pepper to taste and stir in the lemon juice. Pull the dill leaves off the stalks and chop finely. Ladle the soup into 4 individual soup bowls, sprinkle over the dill to garnish and serve immediately.

Avocado soup with quenelles

Exclusive

Serves 4
2 shallots
15 g/½ oz butter
2 ripe avocado pears
juice of ½ lemon
750 ml/1¼ pints vegetable stock
salt
freshly ground white pepper
freshly grated nutmeg
cayenne pepper
250 g/9 oz cod fillet
15 ml/1 tablespoon crème fraîche
1 egg yolk
1 bunch of fresh dill

Approximately per portion:
1,300 kj/310 kcal
13 g protein
27 g fat
2 g carbohydrate

● Approximate preparation
  time: 45 minutes

1. Chop the shallots. Melt the butter in a large saucepan. Add the shallots and fry over a low heat for 2–3 minutes, until soft. Cut the avocado pears in half lengthways, peel and remove the stones. Put the flesh in a food processor and work to make a smooth purée. Mix it with lemon juice to avoid discolouration.

2. Add the avocado purée and vegetable stock to the shallots. Mix thoroughly together, bring to the boil and simmer over a low heat for about 30 minutes. Season to taste with salt, pepper, nutmeg and cayenne pepper.

3. Finely chop the fish and place it in a bowl. Add the crème fraîche and egg yolk and mix thoroughly. Season to taste with salt and pepper. Bring a saucepan of well salted water to the boil. Form the fish mixture into dumplings with a teaspoon, add to the boiling water and cook over a low heat for about 6 minutes.

4. Remove the dill leaves from the stalks and chop finely. Pour the avocado soup into 4 individual soup bowls, divide the quenelles between them, garnish with the chopped dill and serve.

Fish soup with courgettes

Exquisite

Serves 4
800 g/1¾ lb white fish fillets, such
    as cod or haddock
juice of ½ lemon
salt
freshly ground white pepper
1 large onion
25g/1 oz butter
1 garlic clove
½ bunch fresh parsley
250 ml/8 fl oz dry white wine
1 bay leaf
2 cloves
1 litre/1¾ pints vegetable stock
300 g/11 oz courgettes
115 g/4 oz cherry tomatoes
1 bunch fresh basil

Approximately per portion:
1,200 kj/290 kcal
39 g protein
8 g fat
7 g carbohydrate

● Approximate preparation
   time: 1 hour

---

1. Sprinkle the fish fillets with lemon juice and season to taste with salt and pepper. Cover and set aside in the refrigerator.

2. Thinly slice the onion and push out into rings. Melt the butter in a large saucepan. Add the onion and gently fry over a low heat for 2–3 minutes, until it is transparent. Crush the garlic and add it to the saucepan and fry for 1 minute. Pull the parsley leaves off the stalks and finely chop.

3. Add the parsley, white wine, bay leaf and cloves to the saucepan and bring to the boil. Boil over a medium heat until the liquid has reduced by about half. Then add the vegetable stock, bring back to the boil and season to taste with salt and pepper.

4. Cut the courgettes into matchstick strips and stir them into the soup. Cover and cook over a medium heat for about 10 minutes.

5. Blanch the tomatoes in boiling water for 1–2 minutes. Drain and skin them. Cut the fish into bite-size pieces and add it to the soup, together with the tomatoes. Simmer over a low heat for about 8 minutes.

6. Pull off the basil leaves. Ladle the soup into 4 individual soup bowls, garnish with the basil leaves and serve immediately.

Leek and fish soup

Good value

Serves 4
250 g/9 oz floury potatoes
25 g/1 oz butter
500 g/1¼ lb leeks
105 ml/7 tablespoons dry
    white wine
600 ml/1 pint water
salt
freshly ground white pepper
500 g/1¼ lb cod or redfish fillet
juice of ½ lemon
½ bunch fresh dill

Approximately per portion:
1,100 kj/260 kcal
26 g protein
11 g fat
13 g carbohydrate

● Approximate preparation
   time: 45 minutes

---

1. Coarsely grate the potatoes. Melt the butter in a large saucepan. Add the potatoes and fry over a medium heat, stirring frequently, until they are soft.

2. Thinly slice the leeks. Add them to the potatoes and fry, stirring frequently, for 2–3 minutes. Pour in the white wine and water and season to taste with salt and pepper. Bring to the boil and simmer over a medium heat for about 15 minutes.

3. Cut the fish into bite-size pieces. Sprinkle over the lemon juice and season with salt.

4. Pour the soup into a food processor and work to a purée. Return the soup to the saucepan and bring to the boil again. Add the fish pieces, cover and simmer over a low heat for about 5 minutes, until cooked.

5. Meanwhile, pull off the dill leaves from the stalks. Ladle the soup into 4 individual soup bowls, garnish with the dill leaves and serve immediately.

Above: Fish soup with courgettes
Below: Leek and fish soup

Mussels with tomatoes and fennel

Exquisite

Serves 4
2 kg/4½ lb mussels
3 onions
30 ml/2 tablespoons olive oil
4 garlic cloves
1 sprig fresh thyme or 2 teaspoons
  dried thyme
250 ml/8 fl oz dry white wine
250 ml/8 fl oz water
600 g/1 lb 5 oz beef tomatoes
2 fennel heads
salt
freshly ground black pepper
French bread, to serve

Approximately per portion:
930 kj/220 kcal
15 g protein
6 g fat
14 g carbohydrate

● Approximate preparation
   time: 1¼ hours

---

1. Scrub and debeard the mussels under cold running water. Discard any that do not shut immediately when sharply tapped.

2. Chop the onions. Heat the oil in a large saucepan. Add the onions and fry for 3–5 minutes, until soft. Crush the garlic . Add the garlic, thyme, wine and water to the pan and bring to the boil. Add the mussels, cover and simmer over a medium heat for 8–10 minutes, until they have opened. Discard any that remain closed.

3. Remove the mussels from their shells and set aside. Pour the cooking liquid through a strainer lined with muslin into a small saucepan. Bring to the boil and continue boiling until it has reduced by a third.

4. Blanch the tomatoes in boiling water for 1–2 minutes. Drain, skin and coarsely dice the flesh. Add the tomatoes to the saucepan and simmer over a low heat for about 5 minutes.

5. Meanwhile, reserve the feathery fronds that form the fennel tops and finely chop the heads. Add the fennel to the pan and simmer for a further 5 minutes. Chop the fennel tops.

6. Season the sauce well with salt and pepper. Add the mussels and cook over a low heat for about 2 minutes, until warmed through. Transfer to a warmed serving dish, sprinkle over the fennel tops and serve with French bread.

Cod ragoût

Easy to make

Serves 4
2 large leeks
2 onions
4 carrots
2 beef tomatoes
50 g/2 oz butter
salt
freshly ground white pepper
800 g/1¾ lb cod fillets
juice of ½ lemon
3 tablespoons corn oil
mild paprika
1 bunch fresh parsley

Approximately per portion:
1,600 kj/380 kcal
38 g protein
20 g fat
12 g carbohydrate

● Approximate preparation
   time: 50 minutes

---

1. Cut the leeks in half and then into 5 mm/¼ inch wide strips. Finely chop the onions and carrots.

2. Blanch the tomatoes in boiling water for 1–2 minutes. Drain, skin and finely chop the flesh.

3. Melt the butter in a large saucepan. Add the leeks, onions and carrots and fry, stirring frequently, over a low heat for about 10 minutes. Add the tomatoes and season to taste with salt and pepper. Bring to the boil and then simmer over a low heat.

4. Cut the fish into bite-size pieces. Sprinkle with a little salt and the lemon juice. Heat the oil in a frying pan. Add the fish and fry for about 3 minutes, turning it over once. Season with paprika to taste and stir the fish into the pan of vegetables.

5. Pull the parsley leaves off the stalks and chop finely. Transfer the ragoût to a warmed serving dish, sprinkle over the parsley and serve immediately.

Above: Mussels with tomatoes and fennel
Below: Cod ragoût

Fish curry

Exclusive

Serves 4
600 g/1 lb 5 oz cod fillets
juice of ½ lemon
salt
freshly ground white pepper
1 large onion
30 ml/2 tablespoons sunflower oil
1 garlic clove
300 g/11 oz rhubarb
2.5 ml/½ teaspoon sugar
30 ml/2 tablespoons curry powder
350 ml/12 fl oz vegetable stock
105 ml/7 tablespoons double cream
1 bunch fresh flat leaf parsley
boiled brown rice, to serve

Approximately per portion:
1,000 kj/240 kcal
28 g protein
13 g fat
6 g carbohydrate

● Approximate preparation
time: 50 minutes

---

1. Cut the fish into bite-size pieces, sprinkle with about three-quarters of the lemon juice and season with salt and pepper. Cover and set aside in the refrigerator.

2. Finely chop the onion. Heat the oil in a large saucepan. Add the onion and fry over a low heat for 3–5 minutes. Crush the garlic and add it to the pan.

3. Cut the rhubarb into 1 cm/ ½ inch chunks. Add the rhubarb to the pan and fry, stirring occasionally, for about 3 minutes. Sprinkle over the sugar and curry powder. Stir in the vegetable stock. Season to taste with salt and pepper and stir in the remaining lemon juice and the cream. Bring to the boil and simmer over a low heat for about 10 minutes.

4. Pull the parsley leaves off the stalks and finely chop them.

5. Add the fish to the pan and simmer over a low heat for about 5 minutes. Adjust the seasoning, if necessary. Transfer to a warmed serving dish, sprinkle over the parsley and serve with boiled brown rice.

Cod with mangetouts

For beginners

Serves 4
250 g/9 oz mangetouts
250 g/9 oz carrots
25 g/1 oz butter
salt
freshly ground white pepper
400 ml/14 fl oz fish stock
150 ml/¼ pint crème fraîche
5 ml/1 teaspoon cornflour
30 ml/2 tablespoons water
600 g/1 lb 5 oz cod fillets
10 ml/2 teaspoons lemon juice
4 fresh dill sprigs

Approximately per portion:
1,600 kj/380 kcal
31 g protein
23 g fat
11 g carbohydrate

● Approximate preparation
time: 50 minutes

---

1. Cut the mangetouts at an angle into 1 cm/½ inch pieces. Thinly slice the carrots at an angle.

2. Melt the butter in a large frying pan. Add the carrots and stir-fry for 2 minutes. Season to taste with salt and pepper. Add the mangetouts and stir-fry for about 2 minutes.

3. Add the fish stock, bring to the boil and simmer over a medium heat until it has reduced by about one third. Stir in the crème fraîche and simmer over a low heat for about 10 minutes.

4. Mix together the cornflour and water to make a smooth paste. Stir the cornflour mixture into the pan and bring to the boil, stirring constantly, until thickened.

5. Cut the fish into bite-size pieces. Sprinkle over the lemon juice and season with salt and pepper. Add the cod to the pan, cover and simmer over a low heat for about 5 minutes, until cooked through. Pull the dill leaves of the stalks and chop finely. Sprinkle the dill over the fish mixture, transfer to a warmed serving dish and serve immediately.

Above: Fish curry
Below: Cod with mangetouts

Monkfish with grapefruit sauce

Exclusive • Rather expensive

Serves 4
200 g/7 oz carrots
25 g/1 oz butter
2 pink grapefruit
60 ml/4 tablespoons double cream
105 ml/7 tablespoons fish stock
salt
freshly ground white pepper
800 g/1¾ lb monkfish fillets
juice of ½ lemon
15 ml/1 tablespoon corn oil
8 pink grapefruit segments,
    to garnish
boiled wild and long grain rice,
    to serve

Approximately per portion:
1,600 kj/380 kcal
31 g protein
19 g fat
15 g carbohydrate

● Approximate preparation
  time: 30 minutes

---

1. Thinly slice the carrots. Melt half butter in a medium saucepan. Add the carrots and fry, stirring frequently, for about 10 minutes, until soft.

2. Squeeze the juice from both the grapefruit and add it to the carrots in the saucepan.

3. Stir in the cream and fish stock and simmer over a medium heat for about 5 minutes. Transfer the mixture to a food processor and work to form a smooth purée.

Season well with salt and pepper and set aside to keep warm.

4. Cut the fish into chunks and sprinkle with lemon juice. Season with salt and pepper.

5. Heat the remaining butter with the oil in a large frying pan. Add the monkfish chunks and fry for about 5 minutes, turning once. Spoon a little sauce on to 4 individual serving plates and divide the fish between them. Garnish with the pink grapefruit segments and serve with boiled wild and long grain rice.

Fried halibut with paprika

For beginners

Serves 4
600 g/1 lb 5 oz halibut fillets
30 ml/2 tablespoons lemon juice
salt
freshly ground white pepper
500 g/1¼ lb mixed red, yellow and
    green peppers
30 ml/2 tablespoons flour
45 ml/3 tablespoons sunflower oil
2 garlic cloves
105 ml/7 tablespoons dry
    white wine
45 ml/3 tablespoons double cream
15 ml/1 tablespoon tomato paste
mild paprika
5 ml/1 teaspoon dried thyme
5 ml/1 teaspoon oregano
pinch of sugar
fresh oregano and basil sprigs,
    to garnish
boiled rice or warm French bread
    and butter, to serve

Approximately per portion:
1,300 kj/310 kcal
32 g protein
13 g fat
10 g carbohydrate

● Approximate preparation
  time: 35 minutes

---

1. Cut the halibut fillets into bite-size pieces. Sprinkle over the lemon juice and season with salt and pepper.

2. Core and seed the peppers and cut the flesh into thin strips.

3. Put the flour on a plate and roll the fish in it to coat. Discard any surplus flour. Heat the oil in a large frying pan. Fry the fish, stirring gently, for about 1 minute. Remove the fish from the pan, cover and set aside.

4. Add the peppers to the pan and fry for about 3 minutes. Crush the garlic, and add it to the pan. Stir in the white wine, cream and tomato paste. Season to taste with salt, white pepper and paprika and stir in the thyme, oregano and sugar. Cover and cook over a low heat for about 8 minutes.

5. Return the fish to the pan and cook for about 2 minutes, until heated through. Transfer to a serving dish, garnish with the oregano and basil sprigs and serve with rice or warm French bread and butter.

Above: Monkfish with grapefruit sauce
Below: Fried halibut with paprika

Swordfish in coconut sauce

Exclusive • Quick

Serves 4
1 small onion
25 g/1 oz butter
30 ml/2 tablespoons curry powder
250 ml/8 fl oz fish stock
120 ml/4 fl oz double cream
salt
freshly ground white pepper
pinch of sugar
15 ml/1 tablespoon lemon juice
30 ml/2 tablespoons desiccated
   coconut
700 g/1½ lb swordfish fillet
30 ml/2 tablespoons vegetable oil
boiled rice and mixed salad leaves,
   to serve

Approximately per portion:
2,400 kj/570 kcal
35 g protein
45 g fat
8 g carbohydrate

● Approximate preparation
   time: 25 minutes

---

1. Finely chop the onion. Melt the butter in a medium-sized saucepan. Add the onion and fry for about 2–3 minutes, until transparent. Stir in the curry powder.

2. Stir in the fish stock and cream and cook, stirring constantly, over a medium heat for about 5 minutes, until thickened and creamy.

3. Season to taste with salt and pepper and stir in the sugar, lemon juice and coconut. Set aside and keep warm.

4. Cut the fish into 4 slices and season with salt and pepper. Heat the oil in a large frying pan. Add the fish and fry for about 3 minutes on each side, until cooked through.

5. Transfer the fish to 4 warmed individual serving plates and spoon the sauce next to it. Serve with boiled rice and salad leaves.

Plaice with basil sauce

Easy to make

Serves 4
2 bunches fresh basil
250 g/ 9 oz curd cheese
75 ml/5 tablespoons lemon juice
salt
freshly ground white pepper
4 x 400 g/14 oz plaice, cleaned
30–45 ml/2–3 tablespoons flour
115 g/4 oz clarified butter
1 lemon

Approximately per portion:
2,500 kj/600 kcal
77 g protein
26 g fat
10 g carbohydrate

● Approximate preparation
   time: 40 minutes

---

1. Reserve 4 basil sprigs for the garnish and pull the leaves off the stems of the remainder. Put the basil leaves, curd cheese and 45 ml/ 3 tablespoons of the lemon juice in a food processor and work to make a purée. Transfer the purée to a bowl, season to taste with salt and pepper and set aside in the refrigerator.

2. Sprinkle the remaining lemon juice over the plaice and season with salt and pepper.

3. Put the flour in a deep plate and dip the plaice in it, turning to coat completely. Put the fish on a rack to allow the flour to dry.

4. Melt 30 ml/2 tablespoons of the clarified butter in a large frying pan. Add the plaice, in batches if necessary, and fry over a medium heat for 5–6 minutes on each side. Add more clarified butter as necessary and keep the cooked fish warm while you cook the remainder.

5. Cut the lemon into 8 wedges. Put the plaice on 4 individual serving plates, garnish with the lemon and reserved basil sprigs and serve with the basil sauce.

Above: Plaice with basil sauce
Below: Swordfish in coconut sauce

Haddock fillets with courgettes

Easy to make

Serves 4
4 x 150 g/5 oz haddock fillets
juice of ½ lemon
350 g/12 oz courgettes
25 g/1 oz butter
salt
freshly ground black pepper
freshly grated nutmeg
105 ml/7 tablespoons dry
*   white wine*
25 g/1 oz clarified butter
flat leaf parsley sprigs to garnish

Approximately per portion:
1,100 kj/260 kcal
30 g protein
13 g fat
3 g carbohydrate

● Approximate preparation
   time: 50 minutes

---

1. Sprinkle the fish all over with the lemon juice.

2. Thinly slice the courgettes. Melt the butter in a medium saucepan. Add the courgettes and fry, stirring occasionally, for about 5 minutes. Season to taste with salt, pepper and nutmeg.

3. Add the white wine and cook, stirring occasionally, over a medium heat for a further 8 minutes.

4. Melt the clarified butter in a large frying pan. Add the fish and fry for about 2 minutes on each side. Season with salt and pepper.

5. Transfer to 4 warmed individual serving plates, garnish with the parsley and serve immediately with the courgettes.

Variation
You could substitute flat fish fillets, such as lemon sole, brill or dab for the haddock.

Tuna steaks with garlic

Exquisite

Serves 4
1 garlic bulb
2 medium red peppers
3 beef tomatoes
1 small fresh red chilli
1 bunch of fresh coriander or flat
*   leaf parsley*
2.5 ml/½ teaspoon ground cumin
salt
freshly ground white pepper
4 x 175 g/6 oz tuna steaks or slices
45 ml/3 tablespoons clarified butter

Approximately per portion:
2,300 kj/550 kcal
40 g protein
34 g fat
8 g carbohydrate

● Approximate preparation
   time: 2½ hours

---

1. Preheat the oven to 180°C/350°F/Gas 4. Wrap the garlic bulb in aluminium foil and bake in the oven for 45 minutes.

2. Meanwhile, bake the whole peppers in the oven for 20 minutes, turning them over once.

3. Blanch the tomatoes in boiling water for 1–2 minutes. Drain, skin and remove the seeds. Finely chop the tomato flesh. Seed and finely chop the chilli.

4. Remove the peppers from the oven and set aside to cool. When they are cold enough to handle, skin, core and seed the peppers. Finely dice the flesh. mix together the peppers, tomatoes and chilli in a large bowl.

5. Pull the coriander or parsley leaves off their stalks, chop them finely and add to the vegetable mixture. Stir in the cumin and season the mixture to taste with salt and pepper.

6. Remove the garlic from the oven and set aside cool. Squeeze the cloves out of their skins into the vegetable mixture. Mix thoroughly, cover and set aside in the refrigerator for 1 hour.

7. Lightly season the tuna steaks with salt and pepper. Melt the clarified butter in a large frying pan. Add the fish and fry for 2 minutes on each side, until cooked through. Arrange the vegetables with the tuna fish steaks on 4 warmed individual serving plates and serve.

Above: Tuna steaks with garlic
Below: Haddock fillets with courgettes

Special fish cakes with tomatoes

Exquisite

Serves 4
600 g/1 lb 5 oz beef tomatoes
600 g/1 lb 5 oz trout or salmon
fillets
105 ml/7 fl oz crème fraîche
2 eggs
salt
freshly ground white pepper
freshly grated nutmeg
cayenne pepper
2 bunches fresh basil
2 garlic cloves
25 g/1 oz clarified butter
25 g/1 oz butter
French bread, to serve

Approximately per portion:
1,400 kj/330 kcal
32 g protein
22 g fat
6 g carbohydrate

● Approximate preparation
  time: 45 minutes

1. Blanch the tomatoes in boiling water for 1–2 minutes. Drain, skin and cut them into wedges. Put the fish in a food processor and work to make a purée, then transfer to a bowl. Stir in the crème fraîche and the eggs. Season the mixture to taste with salt and pepper and stir in a pinch of nutmeg and a pinch of cayenne pepper.

2. Reserve 4 basil sprigs and pull the remaining leaves off the stalks. Cut half the leaves into thin strips. Crush the garlic and stir it into the fish mixture. Add the strips of basil and mix thoroughly.

3. With damp hands, roll the mixture into balls the size of a tennis ball and then press them flat. Melt the clarified butter in a large frying pan. Add the fish cakes, in batches, and fry over a medium heat for 2 minutes on each side.

4. Meanwhile, melt the butter in another frying pan. Add the tomatoes and fry over a low heat for about 8 minutes. Season to taste with salt and pepper and sprinkle over the whole basil leaves. Arrange the fish cakes and tomatoes on 4 warmed individual serving plates, garnish with the reserved basil sprigs and serve with French bread.

Hake in beer batter

Easy to make • Good value

Serves 4
200 g/7 oz flour
200 ml/7 fl oz light ale
2 eggs
salt
freshly ground white pepper
750 g/1 lb 10 oz hake fillets
1 egg white
6 tablespoons corn oil
1 lemon
parsley sprigs, to garnish
potato salad, lettuce and tartar
   sauce, to serve

Approximately per portion:
2,200 kj/520 kcal
40 g protein
22 g fat
42 g carbohydrate

● Approximate preparation
   time: 45 minutes

Tip

Hake has a very delicate
texture and its flesh is quite
fragile, so it must be handled
with care. This dish would be
equally delicious made with
lemon sole, dab or plaice.

1. Sift the flour into a bowl. Carefully mix in the beer and the eggs until the batter is quite smooth. Season well with salt and pepper. Cover and set aside to stand for 15–20 minutes.

2. Season the fish with salt and pepper, cover and set aside. Stiffly beat the egg white and fold it into the beer batter.

3. Carefully dip the fish fillets in the beer batter to coat. Heat the oil in a large frying pan. Add the fish and fry over a medium heat for 10–15 minutes on each side, until golden and crisp.

4. Slice the lemon. Place the fish on 4 individual serving plates and garnish with the lemon slices and parsley. Serve with potato salad, lettuce and tartar sauce.

Sesame cod

Exquisite

Serves 4
1 small ripe mango
juice of ½ lemon
15 ml/1 tablespoon low-fat
   curd cheese
salt
freshly ground white pepper
cayenne pepper
90 g/3½ oz sesame seeds
750 g/1 lb 10 oz cod fillets
75 ml/5 tablespoons flour
2 eggs
90 ml/6 tablespoons sesame oil
mint sprigs, to garnish

Approximately per portion:
2,100 kj/500 kcal
42 g protein
27 g fat
23 g carbohydrate

● Approximate preparation
  time: 40 minutes

I. Peel the mango and cut the
flesh away from the stone. Put the
mango flesh, 15 ml/1 tablespoon

of the lemon juice and the curd
cheese in a food processor and
work to a purée. Season to taste
with salt, white pepper and
cayenne pepper.

2. Coarsely grind the sesame seeds
in a grinder or in a mortar with a
pestle. Transfer them to a plate.

3. Divide the fish into 4 portions,
sprinkle over the remaining lemon
juice and season to taste with salt
and pepper.

4. Put the flour on a plate. Lightly
beat the eggs. First, dip the fish in
the flour, then in the eggs and,
finally, coat with the ground
sesame seeds.

5. Heat the oil in a large frying pan.
Add the fish and fry over a
medium heat for 4 minutes on
each side, until golden brown.
Transfer the fish to 4 individual
serving plates, spoon the mango
sauce on to the plates, garnish with
the mint sprigs and serve.

Haddock in a Parmesan coating

For guests

Serves 4
750 g/1 lb 10 oz haddock fillets
juice of ½ lemon
salt
freshly ground white pepper
75 ml/5 tablespoons flour
1 egg
150 g/5 oz breadcrumbs
50 g/2 oz freshly grated
   Parmesan cheese
50 g/2 oz finely ground almonds
5 ml/1 teaspoon dried oregano
50 g/2 oz clarified butter
1 lemon
mint sprigs, to garnish
potato and cucumber salad, to serve

Approximately per portion:
2,500 kj/600 kcal
47 g protein • 27 g fat
39 g carbohydrate

● Approximate preparation
  time: 25 minutes

I. Sprinkle the fish with lemon
juice and season with salt and
pepper.

2. Put the flour on a plate. Lightly
beat the egg. Mix together the
breadcrumbs, Parmesan cheese,
almonds and oregano and season
with salt and pepper.

3. Dip the fish in the flour, shaking
off the surplus, then in the beaten
egg and, finally, in the Parmesan
cheese and breadcrumb mixture.
Lightly press the breadcrumb
mixture on to the fish and shake
off the surplus.

4. Melt the clarified butter in a
large frying pan. Add the fish and
fry over a medium heat for
3–4 minutes on each side, until
golden brown.

5. Cut the lemon into 8 wedges.
Transfer the fish to 4 individual
plates, garnish with the lemon
wedges and mint sprigs and serve
with a potato and cucumber salad.

Above: Sesame cod
Below: Haddock in a Parmesan coating

Shark steaks with sherry sauce

Exclusive • Quick

Serves 4
750 g/1 lb 10 oz shark steaks
juice of ½ lemon
salt
freshly ground white pepper
25 g/1 oz butter
1 tablespoon walnut oil
105 ml/7 tablespoons dry sherry
250 ml/8 fl oz double cream
115 g/4 oz chilled butter
boiled wild and long grain rice,
*   to serve*

Approximately per portion:
2,800 kj/670 kcal
39 g protein
53 g fat
3 g carbohydrate

● Approximate preparation
  time: 30 minutes

---

1. Remove the skin and bones from the shark steaks. Sprinkle them with lemon juice and season with salt and pepper.

2. Heat the butter and the oil in a large frying pan. Add the fish and fry over a medium heat for about 3 minutes on each side, until cooked through. Set aside and keep warm.

3. Put the sherry and cream into a medium saucepan, bring to the boil and reduce by about half. Beat in the butter, in small pieces at a time, with a whisk until thoroughly incorporated. Season the sauce with salt and pepper.

4. Arrange the shark steaks on 4 warmed individual plates and pour on the sherry sauce. Serve with boiled wild and long grain rice.

Monkfish saltimbocca

Saltimbocca literally means 'jump into the mouth'.

Exclusive

Serves 4
2 beef tomatoes
800 g/1¾ lb monkfish fillets
juice of ½ lemon
salt
freshly ground white pepper
8 thin slices Parma ham
8 fresh sage leaves
115 g/4 oz butter
300 g/11 oz tagliatelle
1 green courgette
1 yellow courgette

Approximately per portion:
3,100 kj/740 kcal
44 g protein
36 g fat
57 g carbohydrate

● Approximate preparation
  time: 50 minutes

---

1. Blanch the beef tomatoes in boiling water for 1–2 minutes. Drain, skin and seed. Cut one third of the tomato flesh into small cubes and put the remainder in a food processor and work to make a purée.

2. Cut the monkfish into 8 large chunks. Sprinkle over about three quarters of the lemon juice and season with salt and pepper.

3. Lay the fish pieces side by side on a plate. Cover each with 1 slice of ham and 1 sage leaf and secure each with a cocktail stick.

4. Heat half the butter in a large frying pan. Add the monkfish and fry over a medium heat for about 3 minutes on each side. Remove the fish from the frying pan and keep warm.

5. Meanwhile, cook the tagliatelle in lightly salted boiling water for 8 minutes, until tender, but still firm to the bite. Drain well.

6. Slice the courgettes into very thin strips using a vegetable peeler or mandolin.

7. Add the tomato purée to the frying pan and simmer over a low heat until it has reduced by about one third. Season to taste with salt and pepper.

8. Melt the remaining butter in a medium saucepan. Toss in the tagliatelle and courgette strips. Season with salt and pepper and add the remaining lemon juice.

9. Arrange the monkfish saltimbocca on 4 warmed individual serving plates with the tomato sauce and courgette tagliatelle. Sprinkle the tomato cubes over the tagliatelle and serve immediately.

Above: Shark steaks with sherry sauce
Below: Monkfish saltimbocca

Plaice rolls with rocket

Easy to make

Serves 4
600 g/1 lb 5 oz plaice fillets
juice of ½ lemon
salt
freshly ground white pepper
1 small onion
500 g/1¼ lb chanterelle mushrooms
40 g/1½ oz butter
200 ml/7 fl oz dry sherry
90 ml/6 tablespoons crème fraîche
1 bunch rocket (about 65 g/2½ oz)
boiled rice, to serve

Approximately per portion:
1,500 kj/360 kcal
29 g protein
23 g fat
3 g carbohydrate
● Approximate preparation time: 45 minutes

1. Sprinkle the plaice fillets with about three quarters of the lemon juice and season to taste with salt and pepper.

2. Chop the onion. Cut the mushrooms into strips.

3. Melt the butter in a large frying pan. Add the mushrooms and fry for 1 minute. Add the onion and fry for about 5 minutes. Add the sherry and bring to just below the boil. Stir in the crème fraîche and the remaining lemon juice and season to taste with salt and pepper. Cook, stirring occasionally, for a further 5 minutes.

4. Separate the rocket leaves and put 1 or 2 on each plaice fillet.

5. Roll up the fillets, tie them with trussing thread and place them on the mushrooms. Cover and cook over a medium heat for about 10 minutes.

6. Cut the remaining rocket into strips. Transfer the plaice rolls to 4 individual serving plates, remove and discard the trussing thread and scatter over the rocket strips. Spoon the mushroom mixture on to the plates beside the fish rolls and serve with boiled rice.

Haddock dumplings

Exclusive

Serves 4
400 g/14 oz haddock fillets
juice of ½ lemon
2 eggs
150 ml/¼ pint crème fraîche
salt
freshly ground white pepper
250 ml/8 fl oz dry white wine
250 ml/8 fl oz water
1 punnet of cress
4 cherry tomatoes
boiled wild and long grain rice,
   to serve

Approximately per portion:
1,400 kj/330 kcal
24 g protein
20 g fat
4 g carbohydrate
● Approximate preparation time: 1¼ hours

1. Cut the fish into cubes and sprinkle over about half the lemon juice. Separate the eggs and reserve the whites. Put the yolks, fish and half the crème fraîche into a food processor and work to a purée. Beat the egg whites until they are stiff and fold them into the fish mixture. Season with salt and pepper and set aside in the refrigerator to chill for about 30 minutes.

2. Bring the white wine and water to the boil in a large saucepan. Form the fish mixture into dumplings with a teaspoon. Add them to the pan and cook over a low heat for 5–8 minutes. Remove the dumplings with a slotted spoon and keep warm.

3. Boil the cooking liquid over a high heat until it has reduced by half. Stir in the remaining crème fraîche and simmer for a further 5 minutes. Season to taste with salt and pepper and stir in the remaining lemon juice. Return the fish dumplings to the pan and cook for about 3 minutes, until heated through.

4. Transfer the dumplings to 4 individual serving plates. Snip the cress and stir it into the sauce. Pour the sauce over the dumplings. Cut the tomatoes into quarters and arrange them with the fish dumplings and sauce. Serve immediately with boiled wild and long grain rice.

Above: Plaice rolls with rocket
Below: Haddock dumplings

Salmon with asparagus

Quite expensive

Serves 4
1 kg/2¼ lb green asparagus
salt
pinch of sugar
25 g/1 oz butter
2 shallots
250 ml/8 fl oz dry white wine
250 ml/8 fl oz cream
freshly ground white pepper
pinch of cayenne pepper
1–2 bunches chives
250 ml/8 fl oz water
4 x 150 g/5 oz of salmon fillets

Approximately per portion:
2,600 kj/620 kcal
33 g protein
45 g fat
9 g carbohydrate

● Approximate preparation
time: 1 hour

1. Trim and peel the asparagus. Bring a tall saucepan of well salted water to the boil, add the sugar and half the butter. Loosely tie the asparagus stems together, add to the pan, standing upright, and cook for about 15 minutes. Drain and keep warm.

2. Meanwhile, finely chop the shallots. Melt the butter in a medium saucepan. Add the shallots and cook, stirring occasionally, for 3–5 minutes, until soft. Add half the white wine and bring to just below the boil. Pour in the cream and simmer until

thickened and creamy. Season to taste with salt, white pepper and cayenne pepper. Remove the pan from the heat and keep warm.

3. Snip the chives and stir them into the sauce.

4. Bring the remaining white wine and the water to the boil in a large saucepan. Season the salmon fillets to taste with salt and pepper. Add the salmon to the pan and simmer over a low heat for about 8 minutes.

5. Arrange the salmon with the asparagus and the sauce on 4 individual serving plates and serve immediately.

Trout 'au bleu' with lemon sauce

Famous recipe

Serves 4
4 x 400 g/14 oz trout, cleaned
juice of 2 lemons
salt
1 onion
1 bunch fresh parsley
120 ml/4 fl oz vinegar
1 bay leaf
2.5 ml/½ teaspoon peppercorns
1 litre/1¾ pints water
600 g/1 lb 5 oz new potatoes
15 g/½ oz butter
1 bunch fresh dill
3 egg yolks
freshly ground white pepper
dill sprigs, to garnish

Approximately per portion:
2,400 kj/570 kcal
82 g protein
15 g fat
25 g carbohydrate

● Approximate preparation
time: 1 hour

1. Sprinkle the trout with the juice of 1 lemon and season with salt. Tie the heads and tails of the trout together with trussing thread.

2. Cut the onion into quarters. Put the onion, parsley, vinegar, bay leaf, peppercorns and water into a large saucepan. Bring to the boil and simmer for about 20 minutes.

3. Cook the potatoes in lightly salted boiling water for about 20 minutes. Then drain thoroughly. Melt the butter in a frying pan and toss the potatoes into it. Pull the dill leaves off the stalks and sprinkle over the potatoes.

4. Meanwhile, add the trout to the vinegar liquid and simmer over a medium heat for 10–15 minutes.

5. Beat the egg yolks with a pinch of salt in a heat-proof bowl. Place the bowl on another bowl containing hot water. Gradually beat in the remaining lemon juice until thickened and creamy. Season salt and pepper. Transfer the trout to 4 individual serving plates and remove and discard the trussing thread. Spoon the sauce on to the plates, garnish with the dill sprigs and serve with the potatoes.

Above: Trout 'au bleu' with lemon sauce
Below: Salmon with asparagus

Cod parcels

Exquisite

Serves 4
500 g/1¼ lb chard
salt
600 g/1 lb 5 oz cod fillet
juice of ½ lemon
150 ml/¼ pint crème fraîche
freshly ground white pepper
cayenne pepper
2 eggs yolks
25 g/1 oz butter
120 ml/4 fl oz dry white wine

Approximately per portion:
1,500 kj/360 kcal
30 g protein
23 g fat
3 g carbohydrate

● Approximate preparation
 time: 1¼ hours

---

1. Cut off the chard leaves and reserve the stems. Blanch the leaves in lightly salted boiling water for 1 minute. Drain, refresh with cold water and set aside to drain thoroughly.

2. Chop the fish into small pieces. Put it in a bowl and mix in about three quarters of the lemon juice and 60 ml/4 tablespoons of the crème fraîche. Season to taste with salt, white pepper and cayenne pepper. Stir in the egg yolks

3. Spread out 4 chard leaves and divide the fish mixture equally between them. Roll up the leaves, tucking in the sides, and secure with trussing thread.

4. Finely chop the chard stalks. Melt the butter in a frying pan. Add the chard stalks and fry, stirring occasionally, for about 10 minutes, until soft. Add the white wine and bring to just below the boil. Put the chard stalks and the remaining crème fraîche in a food processor and work to a purée. Transfer to a medium saucepan and simmer until the sauce is thickened and creamy. Season with salt and pepper and stir in the remaining lemon juice.

5. Cut the remaining chard leaves into strips and stir them into the sauce. Add the fish parcels, cover and cook over a low heat for about 8–10 minutes. Serve immediately.

Haddock in mustard sauce

Famous recipe

Serves 4
1 onion
1 carrot
1 small head of celery
1 lemon
1 bunch fresh parsley
1 sprig fresh thyme
250 ml/8 fl oz dry white wine
1.5 litres/2½ pints water
2 bay leaves
15 ml/1 tablespoon peppercorns
2 juniper berries
salt
1.2 kg/2 lb 6 oz haddock, cleaned
250 ml/8 fl oz double cream
60 ml/2 tablespoons English
  mustard
3 egg yolks
freshly ground white pepper
pinch of cayenne pepper
1 bunch chives

Approximately per portion:
2,000 kj/480 kcal
53 g protein
22 g fat
8 g carbohydrate

● Approximate preparation
 time: 2 hours

---

1. Dice the onion. Coarsely chop the carrot and celery. Slice the lemon. Put the onion, carrot, celery, lemon, parsley, thyme, wine and water into a large saucepan. Add the bay leaves and peppercorns. Crush the juniper berries and add them to the pan, together with 2.5 ml/½ teaspoon salt. Bring to the boil and simmer for about 20 minutes. Strain and set aside to cool. Discard the flavourings.

2. Put the fish into a large saucepan and add sufficient cold stock to cover. Cook over a low heat, without boiling, for about 30 minutes. Remove the fish from the pan and keep warm.

3. Measure 370 ml/13 fl oz of the cooking liquid into a saucepan. Reserve the remainder. Add the cream to the pan, bring to the boil and cook until reduced by half.

4. Beat the mustard with the egg yolks and 45 ml/3 tablespoons of the reserved cooking liquid. Pour this mixture into the sauce and stir over a low heat, without boiling, until thickened. Season to taste with salt, white pepper and cayenne pepper.

5. Snip the chives and stir into the sauce. Serve the sauce with the fish.

Above: Haddock in mustard sauce
Below: Cod parcels

Turbot fillet in sorrel cream

Exclusive • Expensive

Serves 4
750 g/1 lb 10 oz turbot fillet
freshly ground white pepper
salt
50 g/2 oz fresh sorrel or 2 bunches
* fresh basil*
2 shallots
25 g/1 oz butter
120 ml/4 fl oz fish or
* vegetable stock*
120 ml/4 fl oz dry white wine
200 ml/7 fl oz cream

Approximately per portion:
1,600 kj/380 kcal
33 g protein
25 g fat
3 g carbohydrate

● Approximate preparation
  time: 30 minutes

---

1. Season the turbot fillets with plenty of pepper and a little salt.

2. Cut the sorrel or basil leaves into thin strips.

3. Finely chop the shallots. Melt the butter in a large saucepan. Add the shallots and fry, stirring occasionally, for 3–5 minutes, until soft. Add three quarters of the sorrel or basil and fry for a further 3 minutes.

4. Add the stock and the white wine. Bring to the boil, then lower the heat, so that the liquid is just at simmering point.

5. Add the turbot fillets to the pan and cook for about 1 minute. Remove the turbot from the pan. Transfer to a serving dish, cover and keep warm.

6. Bring the liquid to a vigorous boil again. Add the cream and simmer, over a low heat until the sauce becomes lightly creamy. Season to taste with salt and white pepper.

7. Pour the sorrel cream over the turbot fillets, garnish with the remaining strips of sorrel or basil and serve immediately.

Sole in saffron sauce

Easy to make • Expensive

Serves 4
2 x 400 g/14 oz Dover sole, cleaned
juice of ½ lemon
salt
freshly ground white pepper
1 small onion
1 cucumber
5 g/1 oz butter
2.5 ml/½ teaspoon saffron threads
120 ml/4 fl oz fish stock
30 ml/2 tablespoons crème fraîche
¼ bunch fresh chervil

Approximately per portion:
1,200 kj/290 kcal
36 g protein
13 g fat
4 g carbohydrate

● Approximate preparation
  time: 40 minutes

---

1. Sprinkle the sole with about three quarters of the lemon juice and season with salt and pepper.

2. Finely chop the onion. Peel the cucumber, cut it in half lengthways and remove the seeds. Cut the cucumber into 1 cm/½ inch cubes.

3. Melt the butter in a large saucepan. Add the onion and cucumber and fry for 3–5 minutes, until the onion is soft. Crush the saffron and sprinkle over the onion and cucumber. Cook, stirring constantly until the mixture is golden brown. Add the fish stock, stir in the crème fraîche and season to taste with salt and pepper.

4. Bring the mixture to the boil. Place the sole in the boiling liquid, remove the pan from the heat, cover and leave the fish to cook for 5–6 minutes. Transfer the fish to a work surface, skin and lift the flesh from the bones into a serving dish.

5. Pull the chervil leaves off the stems. Season the sauce with salt and pepper and stir in the remaining lemon juice. Pour the sauce over the fish, scatter over the chervil leaves and serve.

Above: Turbot fillet in sorrel cream
Below: Sole in saffron sauce

Conger eel on a bed of vegetables

For beginners

Serves 4
400 g/14 oz leeks
700 g/1½ lb floury potatoes, such
   as Maris Piper
250 g/ 9 oz mushrooms
15 g/½ oz butter
15 ml/1 tablespoon corn oil
salt
freshly ground black pepper
2.5 ml/½ teaspoon dried marjoram
250 ml/8 fl oz vegetable stock
750 g/1 lb 10 oz eel cutlets
juice of ½ lemon

Approximately per portion:
3,000 kj/710 kcal
34 g protein
52 g fat
29 g fat

● Approximate preparation
   time: 50 minutes

---

1. Cut the leeks, diagonally into
5 mm/¼ inch slanted pieces.

2. Cut the potatoes into 1 cm/
½ inch cubes. Thinly slice the
mushrooms.

3. Heat the butter and oil in a
large saucepan. Add the leeks and
potatoes and fry over a high heat
for 3 minutes. Season to taste with
salt and pepper and add the
marjoram and vegetable stock. Half
cover the saucepan and simmer
over a low heat for 5 minutes.

4. Sprinkle the eel cutlets with
lemon juice and season with salt
and pepper. Add these to pan,
cover and simmer over a low heat
for about 10–12 minutes, until
cooked. Remove the eel from the
pan. Spoon the vegetables on to
4 individual serving plates, top with
the eel cutlets and serve.

Carp 'au bleu'

Famous recipe

Serves 4
1 onion
1 carrot
1 small head of celery
1 leek
1 bunch fresh flat leaf parsley
1 litre/1¾ pints water
2 bay leaves
5 ml/1 teaspoon allspice berries
5 ml/1 teaspoon peppercorns
salt
250 ml/8 fl oz white wine vinegar
1.2 kg/2 lb 10 oz carp, cleaned
freshly ground white pepper
juice of ½ lemon
1 thick slice of fresh white bread
250 ml/8 fl oz beef stock
rind of 1 lemon
120 ml/4 fl oz double cream
30–45 ml/ 2–3 tablespoons grated
   fresh horseradish or
   creamed horseradish
freshly grated nutmeg

Approximately per portion:
2,000 kj/480 kcal
53 g protein
24 g fat
11 g carbohydrate

● Approximate preparation
   time: 1 hour

---

1. Coarsely chop the onion, carrot
and celery. Slice the leek
lengthways into broad strips.

2. Put the onion, carrot, celery,
leek and parsley into a large
saucepan. Add the water, 1 bay
leaf, the allspice berries,
peppercorns, 5 ml/1 teaspoon salt
and the vinegar. Bring to the boil
and simmer over a low heat for
about 20 minutes.

3. Season the inside of the carp
with salt and rub three quarters of
the lemon juice over it. Add the
carp to the saucepan, cover and
cook over a low heat for about
25–30 minutes.

4. Meanwhile, remove and discard
the crusts from the bread and
crumble it into the stock. Put the
stock, the remaining bay leaf and
the lemon rind into a medium
saucepan. Pour in the cream and
simmer over a low heat until the
sauce has thickened.

5. Remove the lemon rind and the
bay leaf. Stir in the grated
horseradish or horseradish cream
and the remaining lemon juice and
season to taste with salt, pepper
and nutmeg. Serve the sauce with
the carp.

Above: Carp 'au bleu'
Below: Conger eel on a bed of vegetables

Haddock fillets with mushroom sauce

This easy recipe will work successfully with most white fish.

For beginners

Serves 4
2 onions
500 g/1¼ lb mushrooms
juice of ½ lemon
40 g/1½ oz butter, plus extra, for greasing
1 bunch fresh flat leaf parsley
200 g/7 oz full-fat cream cheese with herbs
60 ml/4 tablespoons double cream
2 garlic cloves
salt
freshly ground white pepper
1 egg yolk
800 g/1¾ lb haddock fillets

Approximately per portion:
2,400 kj/570 kcal
47 g protein
40 g fat
5 g carbohydrate

● Approximate preparation time: 1 hour

1. Finely chop the onions. Thinly slice the mushrooms and sprinkle over half the lemon juice. Preheat the oven to 220°C/425°F/Gas 7.

2. Melt the butter in a large frying pan. Add the onions and fry for 1–2 minutes, until they become transparent. Add the mushrooms and fry for 2 minutes.

3. Meanwhile, pull the parsley leaves off the stalks and chop finely. Add the parsley, cream cheese and cream to the pan. Crush the garlic and add to the pan. Bring to the boil, then remove the pan from the heat.

4. Season the mushroom mixture to taste with salt and white pepper and stir in about 5 ml/1 teaspoon of the remaining lemon juice. Set aside to cool. Lightly beat the egg yolk and fold it into the mushroom mixture.

5. Sprinkle the fish with the remaining lemon juice and season with salt and pepper. Grease an ovenproof dish. Arrange the fish on the base of the dish and spread the mushroom mixture on top. Bake in the middle of the oven for about 10 minutes. Turn off the oven and leave the fish to continue cooking for a further 5 minutes before serving.

Pollack Florentine

Easy to make

Serves 4
1 kg/2¼ lb leaf spinach
1 large onion
4 garlic cloves
25 g/1 oz butter, plus extra, for greasing
60 ml/4 tablespoons mascarpone cheese
salt
freshly ground black pepper
freshly grated nutmeg
4 x 185 g/6½ oz pollack cutlets
½ bunch fresh flat leaf parsley
1 lemon

Approximately per portion:
1,200 kj/290 kcal
41 g protein
12 g fat
5 g carbohydrate

● Approximate preparation time: 1 hour

1. Trim the spinach leaves.

2. Finely chop the onion. Melt the butter in a large saucepan. Add the onion and fry for 3–5 minutes, until soft. Crush and add 2 of the garlic cloves.

3. Add the spinach. Cover the pan and cook for about 5 minutes, until the spinach wilts. Stir in the mascarpone cheese. Season to taste with salt, pepper and nutmeg. Preheat the oven to 220°C/425°F/Gas 7.

4. Season the pollack cutlets with salt and pepper. Crush the remaining garlic cloves and spread over the fish.

5. Grease an ovenproof dish and spoon the spinach mixture over the base. Arrange the pollack cutlets on top.

6. Lay the parsley on the fish. Thinly slice the lemon and arrange the slices on the fish. Cover and bake in the middle of the oven for about 20 minutes, until cooked through. Serve immediately.

Above: Haddock fillets with mushroom sauce
Below: Pollack Florentine

Salmon trout in a herby salt coating

Exquisite

Serves 4
2 kg/4½ lb sea salt
5 ml/1 teaspoon dried rosemary
5 ml/1 teaspoon dried thyme
5 ml/1 teaspoon dried oregano
4 garlic cloves
1.2 kg/2 lb 10 oz salmon trout, cleaned
freshly ground white pepper
1 bunch fresh coriander or flat leaf parsley
boiled potatoes and lemon mayonnaise, to serve

Approximately per portion:
1,100 kj/260 kcal
49 g protein
7 g fat
0 g carbohydrate

● Approximate preparation time: 1 hour

---

1. Preheat the oven to 240°C/ 475°F/Gas 9. In a bowl, mix together the sea salt, rosemary, thyme and oregano. Crush the garlic and stir it into the mixture.

2. Sprinkle a little herb-flavoured salt inside the fish and season the inside with pepper. Place the coriander over the fish.

3. Spread half the herb-flavoured salt on the base of a large ovenproof dish. Place the fish on it and cover with the remaining salt.

4. Bake the salmon trout in the oven for about 25 minutes. Turn off the oven and leave the fish to continue cooking for a further 10 minutes.

5. Carefully break away the salt crust and transfer the salmon trout to a plate. Remove and discard the head, tail and skin. Lift the fillets off the bone and transfer to individual serving plates. Serve with boiled potatoes and a lemon mayonnaise.

Red mullet on a bed of piquant cabbage

Quite expensive

Serves 4
1 bunch fresh basil or parsley
4 x 250 g/9 oz red mullet, cleaned
50 g/2 oz butter
3 garlic cloves
salt
freshly ground white pepper
15 ml/1 tablespoon lemon juice
1 cabbage (about 500 g/1¼ lb)
1 large onion
30 ml/2 tablespoons clarified butter
250 ml/8 fl oz dry white wine

Approximately per portion:
2100 kj/500 kcal
52 g protein
24 g fat
9 g carbohydrate

● Approximate preparation time: 1½–2 hours

---

1. Reserve a few basil sprigs for the garnish. Put the remainder inside each fish.

2. Cream 40 g/1½ oz of the butter with a fork. Crush the garlic and mash it into the butter. Season with salt and pepper and mix in the lemon juice. Divide the flavoured butter between the cavities of the fish.

3. Shred the cabbage. Thinly slice the onion and push out into rings. Melt the clarified butter in a flameproof baking dish. Add the onion and fry for 3 minutes. Add the cabbage and fry, stirring frequently, for about 10 minutes. Preheat the oven to 180°C/ 350°F/Gas 4.

4. Add the white wine and season with salt and pepper. Arrange the fish on top, dot it with the remaining butter and cook in the middle of the oven for about 50 minutes.

5. To test whether it is cooked press a fork into the fish. If the flesh is firm, it is ready. Serve immediately, garnished with the reserved basil sprigs.

Tip

This dish is best made with leafy spring cabbage, but this is not available all the year round. You can use Savoy cabbage or white cabbage instead.

Above: Salmon trout in a herby salt coating
Below: Red mullet on a bed of piquant cabbage

Baked mackerel with basil butter

For beginners

Serves 4
2 bunches fresh basil
3–4 garlic cloves
75 g/3 oz butter
salt
freshly ground black pepper
4 x 300g/11 oz mackerel, cleaned
juice of 1 lemon
boiled potatoes and mixed salad
    leaves, to serve

Approximately per portion:
2,600 kj/620 kcal
48 g protein
48 g fat
2 g carbohydrate

● Approximate preparation
  time: 45 minutes

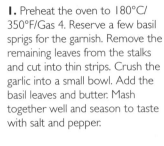

1. Preheat the oven to 180°C/ 350°F/Gas 4. Reserve a few basil sprigs for the garnish. Remove the remaining leaves from the stalks and cut into thin strips. Crush the garlic into a small bowl. Add the basil leaves and butter. Mash together well and season to taste with salt and pepper.

2. Sprinkle the mackerel, inside and out, with lemon juice and season with salt and pepper.

3. Divide the basil-flavoured butter between the cavities of the fish. Wrap 2 mackerel together in a large piece of aluminium foil, folding the edges over to seal. Cook the fish parcels in the middle of the oven for 25–30 minutes.

4. Carefully remove the fish from the foil. Remove and discard the heads, skin and bones. Arrange the mackerel on 4 individual warmed plates and pour over the cooking juices. Garnish with the reserved basil sprigs and serve with boiled potatoes and mixed salad leaves.

Prawns with grated cheese and mushrooms

For guests •
Rather time-consuming

Serves 4
600 g/1 lb 5 oz raw prawns, fresh
* or frozen*
juice of ½ lemon
salt
freshly ground white pepper
2 small onions
30 ml/2 tablespoons sesame oil
2 garlic cloves
250 g/9 oz mushrooms
200 g/7 oz carrots
200 g/7 oz courgettes
5 ml/1 teaspoon dried thyme
250 ml/8 fl oz vegetable stock
60 ml/4 tablespoons crème fraîche
50 g/2 oz Parmesan cheese,
* freshly grated*
butter for greasing
fresh coriander or flat leaf parsley
* sprigs, to garnish*

Approximately per portion:
1,400 kj/330 kcal
32 g protein
19 g fat
6 g carbohydrate

● Approximate preparation
   time: 1 hour 10 minutes

1. Thaw the prawns if frozen. Peel and devein the prawns, sprinkle with lemon juice and season with salt and pepper. Cover and set aside in the refrigerator.

2. Finely dice the onions. Heat the oil in a large saucepan. Add the onions and fry, stirring occasionally, for 3–5 minutes, until soft. Crush the garlic and add it to the pan. Slice the mushrooms and add to the pan. Preheat the oven to 220°C/425°/Gas 7.

3. Coarsely grate the carrots and courgettes into the saucepan. Fry, stirring frequently, for about 2 minutes. Season with salt and pepper and stir in the thyme. Add the vegetable stock, bring to the boil, then lower the heat and simmer until reduced by a third.

4. Grease an ovenproof dish. Spoon half the vegetable mixture into the base and arrange the prawns on top. Combine the remaining vegetable mixture with the crème fraîche and the Parmesan cheese and spread over the prawns. Bake in the middle of the oven for about 20 minutes. until the top is golden brown. Garnish with the coriander or parsley sprigs and serve.

Salmon trout with summer vegetables

For guests

Serves 4
2 small onions
2 small courgettes (each about 115 g/4 oz)
4 tomatoes
15 ml/1 tablespoon olive oil
120 ml/4 fl oz white wine
salt
freshly ground black pepper
800 g/1¾ lb salmon trout fillet
juice of ½ lemon
20 ml/4 teaspoons butter, plus extra for greasing
boiled potatoes, to serve

Approximately per portion:
1,400 kj/330 kcal
41 g protein
14 g fat
6 g carbohydrate

● Approximate preparation time: 45 minutes

---

1. Thinly slice the onions and push out into rings. Coarsely grate the courgettes. Blanch the tomatoes in boiling water for 1–2 minutes. Drain, skin and quarter them. Preheat the oven to 240°C/475°F/Gas 9.

2. Heat the olive oil in a large frying pan. Add the onions and courgettes and fry, stirring occasionally, for 3–5 minutes. Pour in the white wine, season with salt and pepper and cook over a low heat for about 10 minutes.

3. Divide the fish into 4 portions, sprinkle with lemon juice and season with salt and pepper. Grease an ovenproof dish and arrange the fish in it. Dot 5 ml/1 teaspoon butter on to each portion. Cook in the middle of the oven for about 4 minutes. Add the tomatoes to the dish, return to the oven and cook for a further 4 minutes.

4. Arrange the fish on 4 individual plates and serve with the onion and courgette mixture, the tomatoes and boiled new potatoes.

Fish with herbs

Exclusive

Serves 4
1 freshwater fish, such as zander or tilapia, cleaned (about 1 kg/ 2¼ lb)
salt
freshly ground white pepper
1 bunch spring onions
2 carrots
1 fresh thyme sprig
1 fresh rosemary sprig
1 bunch fresh flat leaf parsley
1 bay leaf
250 ml/8 fl oz dry white wine
250 ml/8 fl oz vegetable stock
5 ml/1 teaspoon peppercorns
150 g/5 oz chilled butter
15 ml/1 tablespoon lemon juice

Approximately per portion:
2,300 kj/550 kcal
45 g protein
33 g fat
7 g carbohydrate

● Approximate preparation time: 1 hour

---

1. Season the fish with salt and pepper.

2. Thinly slice the spring onions into rings. Stuff half of them into the fish.

3. Cut the carrots into slices 5 mm/¼ inch thick. Put the thyme, rosemary, parsley, the remaining spring onions, the carrots and bay leaf into a large saucepan. Pour in the white wine and the vegetable stock and add 5 ml/1 teaspoon salt and the peppercorns. Bring to the boil, lower the heat and simmer for about 10 minutes.

4. Preheat the oven to 180°C/350°F/Gas 4. Put the fish in a baking dish and pour the hot stock over it. Cover the dish and cook in the middle of the oven for 20–30 minutes.

5. The fish is ready when the gills come off easily. Remove the fish from the cooking liquid, set aside and keep warm.

6. Strain the cooking liquid into a saucepan and discard the flavourings. Bring to the boil and cook until it has reduced by about one third. Dice the butter and vigorously beat it into the sauce, one piece at a time, until thickened and creamy. Do not allow the sauce to boil again. Season to taste with salt and pepper and stir in the lemon juice.

7. Skin the fish and remove the bones. Serve with the sauce.

Above: Fish with herbs
Below: Salmon trout with summer vegetables

Halibut parcels

Easy to make

Serves 4
4 x 200 g/7 oz halibut steaks
juice of ½ lemon
salt
freshly ground white pepper
1 small onion
15 ml/1 tablespoon sunflower oil
15 ml/1 tablespoon sesame seed oil
2 garlic cloves
1 cm/½ inch piece fresh root ginger
150 g/5 oz carrots
150 g/5 oz sugar-snap peas
250 g/9 oz beansprouts
30 ml/2 tablespoons soy sauce
30 ml/2 tablespoons dry sherry

Approximately per portion:
1,300 kj/310 kcal
46 g protein
10 g fat
11 g carbohydrate

● Approximate preparation
  time: 45 minutes

---

1. Sprinkle the halibut with the lemon juice and season with salt and pepper.

2. Finely chop the onion. Heat the sunflower and sesame oils in a frying pan. Add the onion and fry for 3–5 minutes, until soft. Crush the garlic and add it to the pan. Finely dice the ginger and add it to the pan. Preheat the oven to 180°C/350°F/Gas 4.

3. Coarsely grate the carrots. Slice the sugar-snap peas diagonally into 2 cm/¾ inch long, slanted pieces.

4. Add the carrots, sugar-snap peas and beansprouts to the frying pan and pour in the soy sauce and sherry. Season well with salt and pepper. Cover and braise over a low heat for about 8 minutes.

5. Cut 4 pieces of aluminium foil large enough to enclose the halibut steaks. Divide the vegetables and fish between them, wrap the foil loosely and fold the edges over to seal. Put the parcels on a baking sheet and cook the fish in the middle of the oven for 10–15 minutes.

6. Remove the baking sheet and carefully transfer the parcels to 4 warmed individual serving dishes. Loosen the foil, but do not unwrap, and serve immediately.

Sea bream on a bed of fennel and potatoes

Easy to make

Serves 4
600 g/1 lb 5 oz fennel
800 g/1¾ lb equal-sized floury
* potatoes, such as Maris Piper*
* or Catriona*
30 ml/2 tablespoons olive oil
salt
freshly ground black pepper
1 bunch fresh thyme
250 ml/8 fl oz white wine
250 g/9 oz mascarpone cheese
2 x 600 g/1 lb 5 oz sea
* bream, cleaned*
5 ml/1 teaspoon anise
1 lemon

Approximately per portion:
2,600 kj/620 kcal
65 g protein
18 g fat
38 g carbohydrate

● Approximate preparation
  time: 1¼ hours

---

1. Cut off the feathery green fronds from the fennel bulbs and reserve. Cut the bulbs into thin slices. Thinly slice the potatoes. Preheat the oven to 200°C/400°F/Gas 6.

2. Brush an ovenproof dish with the oil. Arrange the fennel and potatoes alternately in overlapping rows and season to taste.

3. Pull half the thyme leaves off the stalks and sprinkle over the vegetables. Mix together the white wine and the mascarpone cheese with a hand-held electric whisk and pour the mixture over the vegetables. Cover with aluminium foil and cook them in the middle of the oven for about 30 minutes.

4. Season the fish with salt and pepper and stuff them with the fennel fronds, anise and the remaining thyme. Slice the lemon.

5. Reduce the oven temperature to 180°C/350°F/Gas 4. Remove the aluminium foil and place the fish on the vegetables. Put the lemon slices on top. Return to the oven and cook for about 30 minutes. Serve immediately.

Above: Sea bream on a bed of fennel and potatoes
Below: Halibut parcels

Great Little Cook Books
Fish

Published originally under the title
Fisch und Meeresfrüchte by Gräfe
und Unzer Verlag GmbH,
München

© 1990 by Gräfe und Unzer Verlag
GmbH, München

English-language edition
© 1998 by Transedition Limited,
Oxford, England

This edition published by
Aura Books plc

Translation:
Translate-A-Book, Oxford

Editing:
Linda Doeser

Typesetting:
Organ Graphic, Abingdon

10 9 8 7 6 5 4 3 2 1
Printed in Dubai

ISBN 1 901683 36 2

Note:
Quantities for all recipes are given
in both metric and imperial
measures and, if appropriate, in
standard measuring spoons. They
are not interchangeable, so readers
should follow one set or the other.
5 ml = 1 teaspoon
15 ml = 1 tablespoon

Cornelia Adam
initially worked as a professional
hotelier. Later she took her wide
experience abroad on professional
trips as the editor of a famous
illustrated women's magazine. For
some time now she has worked as
a freelance food journalist and
cookery writer.

Odette Teubner
was taught by her father, the
internationally renowned food
photographer, Christian Teubner.
Later, she worked for some
months as a fashion photographer.
Now she works exclusively in the
Teubner Studio for Food
Photography. In her spare time she
is an enthusiastic painter of
children's portraits. She uses her
own son as a model.

Dorothee Gödert
After finishing her studies, she
started work as a photographer of
still life and interiors. After a visit
to Princeton in the United States,
she specialized in food
photography. She has worked with
several well-known food
photographers and has been
working in the Teubner Studio
since April 1988.